NATIONAL
EXPRESS COACHES

KEITH A. JENKINSON

First published 2017

Amberley Publishing
The Hill, Stroud
Gloucestershire, GL5 4EP

www.amberley-books.com

Copyright © Keith A. Jenkinson, 2017

The right of Keith A. Jenkinson to be identified
as the Author of this work has been asserted
in accordance with the Copyright, Designs and
Patents Act 1988.

ISBN 978 1 4456 7877 1 (print)
ISBN 978 1 4456 7878 8 (ebook)

British Library Cataloguing in Publication Data.
A catalogue record for this book is available from
the British Library.

Origination by Amberley Publishing.
Printed in the UK.

Introduction

The white-liveried coaches of National Express have been a familiar sight throughout England and Wales for forty-five years, as well as in Scotland for around three decades, and in this book I have attempted to show the numerous changes along the way.

Born from the National Bus Company in 1972, for many years National Express owned only one coach of its own, with all the others on its services being provided by other National Bus Company operators but painted in the corporate white livery. At busy times it was common to see non-corporate-liveried coaches providing assistance, and independent operators were often used to provide the additional coaches needed. Although today National Express maintains its own fleet of around 100 coaches to uphold its daily service network, it still relies largely on contracted independent companies to provide all the other vehicles – almost all of which are to National Express specification and wear its corporate livery and identity. On occasions, however, its own coaches are temporarily adorned with promotional logos and so on, and these are to be seen within these pages, together with an assortment of independent coaches that have been used across the years.

In addition to its UK coaching activities, National Express Group also owns a number of companies on mainland Europe, as well as some bus operators in the UK, and has dabbled in railways. However, as none of these are within the remit of this book, they are not included.

Although the majority of the following photographs have been taken by myself, without the generous help of others it would not have been possible to illustrate some parts of National Express' history, and to those people I offer my sincere thanks. Where known, each image has been credited in the caption but unfortunately others remain unidentified. To the latter, I hope they will accept my apologies and forgive me for using their photographs, but will enjoy seeing their work in print.

Keith A. Jenkinson
Queensbury, 2017

National Express Coaches

Although today the National Express Group is a global public limited company that operates buses and trains on three continents, its foundations date back to 1 April 1972 when the state-owned National Bus Company (NBC) created its Central Activities Group – a body that assumed responsibility for all of its various leisure product interests.

Soon after its birth on 1 January 1969, following the merging of the British Electric Traction (BET) and Transport Holding Company (THC) into a single group, the National Bus Company quickly found itself in a chaotic position as far as its express coach services were concerned, with numerous former BET services running in direct competition with those operated by the old THC subsidiaries. Such a situation was both wasteful in terms of vehicles and staff, and non-profitable in economic terms. As a consequence, a study was undertaken as to how best rationalisation could be achieved. Although it was obvious that a solution could not be arrived at overnight, plans began to be formulated, which, in addition to eliminating self-competition, were believed would lead to greater profitability and an improved service network from which the travelling public would ultimately benefit. The only way forward appeared to be the setting up of a separate management team who could control the operation centrally instead of leaving it in the hands of various NBC subsidiaries, as had been the case in the past, and to this end the Central Activities Group (CAG) was created on 1 April 1972. The responsibility of the new body was the creation and profitable operation of a national network of long-distance express coach services, tours and inclusive holidays in Britain and Europe, as well as major charter work, sales outlets and overseas developments by the integration of the planning and the marketing of comparable services of the individual NBC subsidiaries. In addition, the new Central Activities Group also assumed responsibility for the operation of those NBC companies that were solely engaged in coach operations. One of the first priorities was to gain public awareness of the NBC's coaching activities as a whole. In a bid to achieve this goal, it was agreed that a new corporate livery should be established, into which all the NBC subsidiaries would repaint their coaches, and that this must be eyecatching at long distances. After much deliberation, the design consultancy who had been appointed to conceive a corporate scheme recommended one of overall bright yellow, but after giving this an amount of consideration the powers that be within the NBC rejected it on the grounds that it could be easily confused with the livery used by a well-known national building contractor (Wimpey). After further thought, the design consultancy suggested an all-white scheme that, it stated, would be distinctive, tasteful and instantly recognised. To further portray a corporate image, it was agreed that a new standard fleet name should be applied to all the repainted coaches, and after considering a variety of suggestions the name chosen was simply 'NATIONAL', which was to be applied on each side of the coach in large, alternating red and blue letters, accompanied by NBC's 'double-N' symbol, which should always be forward pointing. The first coach to be thus treated was a Bristol RELH of Eastern Counties Omnibus Co.

At this time, the coaches owned by the various NBC subsidiaries were anything but standardised, reflecting pre-NBC buying policies, and included numerous elderly vehicles that were due for early replacement. Among the chassis manufacturers represented were AEC, Bedford, Bristol and Leyland, while bodywork was even more varied with Alexander, Duple, Harrington, Plaxton and Willowbrook, as well as a few others being featured, and it quickly became a priority to start a vehicle replacement programme to fit the new National image.

Among the first major decisions to emerge from the new CAG was to delegate the day-to-day responsibilities to five regional National Travel coach managers who would be able to quickly respond to local requirements and keep a close connection with the various individual NBC operating companies. It was therefore decided during 1973 to set up five regional companies under the National Travel title: National Travel (Midlands) Ltd, which was formed by the renaming of South Midland Motor Services Ltd on 7 December 1973, and a month later acquired independent coach operators Don Everall Travel, Wolverhampton, and Worthington Motor Tours of Birmingham; National Travel (North East) Ltd, which assumed control of Hebble Motor Services and Sheffield United Tours from 1 January 1974; National Travel (South East) Ltd, which came into being in January when it took charge of London Coastal Coaches, Timpsons, Samuelsons and Tillings; National Travel (North West) Ltd, which took over North Western Road Car Co. from 6 February 1974 and who, since March 1972, had been purely an express service and coach operator and held responsibility for wholly owned subsidiaries W. C. Standerwick and Scout Computer Services; and National Travel (South West) Ltd, which was born from Black & White Motorways Ltd on 11 February 1974 and was joined by Greenslades and Shamrock & Rambler. Once this transformation had been completed, attention was turned towards bringing it to the notice of the public, and in a bid to gain greater awareness a massive publicity campaign was launched in the national and local press, as well as on television. To highlight this, a cartoon-type drawing of a coach was created, which was affectionately given the name 'Willie Whitecoach', and soon both children and adults alike began to associate themselves with this gimmick.

During the period of adjustment following the formation of National Travel, express coach services had continued in much the same way as they had done since the NBC had taken control in 1969, despite various attempts to co-ordinate the routes operated by the various NBC regional subsidiaries. On 1 October 1973, however, it was decided to market all the Central Activity Group's services under the trading name of 'National Travel', although plans were already well in hand to adopt a number of brand names such as 'National Express', 'National Charter' and 'National Holidays' so as to easily differentiate between the varying natures of these particular NBC activities (though none of these would be operators in their own right, nor own any coaches, as their sole function was to be for marketing and publicity). At this time, all the road service licences remained in the hands of the companies to whom they had been issued, though it had been made known that these would ultimately be transferred to the new regional National Travel companies, and that all the express services would be renumbered into a single series to assist the travelling public in more easily identifying them. Meanwhile, as the National Travel companies had insufficient vehicles with which to operate their newly acquired duties, coaches would largely be provided by NBC's subsidiary companies, who would be paid on a mileage basis by National Travel, and this in turn would fully utilise these subsidiaries' coaching assets. In addition, the Central Activities Group entered into a 50/50 agreement with a United Dominions Trust car hire company in March 1973, which it then branded Swan National and operated from a number of NBC bus and coach subsidiary bases. However, despite its success, the powers that be within the NBC ultimately decreed that its 50 per cent investment should be sold to its partner and thus this venture sadly came to an end in 1979.

As it made no sense to have operators within the Group offering similar express services or holiday tours, to this end the latter was divorced from the express operations by the creation of a separate division under the title of 'National Holidays', which took over the tours programmes offered by the various NBC subsidiaries and consolidated them into a single brochure, in which several references were initially made to the 'old' operators so that customers were still able to associate themselves with the quality to which they had been accustomed. Additionally, the Europabus operations in which National Travel were actively involved were expanded to include new destinations, although for their share of the service the Plaxton-bodied Bristol RELHs that National Travel (South East) provided were considered to be below the standard of other operators and, despite having air conditioning and a refrigerator, lacked an on-board toilet. To address this, National Travel (South East) purchased four new left-hand drive AEC Reliances for use on the continent in 1974, one of which operated on the long service to Greece.

Later, on 19 May 1974, Eastern National transferred its remaining coach operations to National Travel (South East), one of whose activities was to contract a number of its coaches to various tour operators, including Global and Frames, and paint them in these company's distinctive liveries. Additionally, the business of Wessex Coaches of Bristol was acquired and absorbed into National Travel (South West) on 1 August under the title 'Wessex National'. Before leaving 1974, mention must be made of the purchase by National Travel (South West) of a Bristol Omnibus Co. Lodekka, which, after being suitably modified and painted into National white livery, was dispatched to the Aust service area interchange near the Severn Bridge on the M4 motorway, where it replaced a former Red & White Bristol MW single-decker as a booking office and waiting room.

1975 began with the transfer of Eastern Counties Omnibus Co.'s Norwich-based Mascot National coaching operations to National Travel (South East) on 1 January, together with four Duple-bodied Bedford YRT coaches that were to leave

Eastern Counties to continue its other long-established express activities. Then, in an attempt to attract more passengers onto its London services, National Travel (South East) inaugurated a new link service to connect Victoria Coach Station with Victoria railway station using a Ford Transit minicoach. However, not being widely used, it did not last long and was ultimately discontinued. Meanwhile, National Travel began a new service from London to Galway in Ireland, which used B&I Lines ferries from Liverpool to Dun Laoghaire and was operated jointly with Ireland's national transport operator, CIE. Then, before the year ended, National Travel (South East) took delivery of a special vehicle based on a Leyland National bus. Purchased for use by the NBC, it had been specially modified (while under construction) to become what can best be described as a mobile conference room with full office facilities and a small servery. Although meant for use by executives requiring these facilities while travelling, it sadly saw little use and remained a one-off within National Travel's empire. It was not, however, the only unusual vehicle to be purchased in 1975, as National Travel (South East) also acquired a former East Kent Road Car Co. open-top Park Royal-bodied AEC Regent V, which was repainted into corporate white livery and was used on private hire and celebratory events. Meanwhile, two of South East's Leyland Leopard coaches were given Seaspeed livery for use on services between London and Kent ports, followed a year later by two AEC Reliances being given Hoverlloyd colours and branding for use on similar services.

The upgrading of National Travel's fleet continued apace and it was decided in 1976 to withdraw the double-deck Bristol VRLLH coaches that were operated by National Travel (North West) and to maintain its services with single-deckers in the future. A few special liveries continued to appear for tour companies and ferry operators, and in 1977 two National Travel (South East) coaches were given London Transport's familiar red livery for use on tours and excursions that were organised by LTE and marketed in conjunction with National Travel. Meanwhile, to commemorate the Silver Jubilee of HM Queen Elizabeth II, the open-top AEC Regent V of National Travel (South East) was repainted in a silver livery with appropriate lettering for use on a wide variety of duties throughout the summer months. Prior to this, on 1 April, National Travel (South East) purchased the old established London to Clacton service of Beeline jointly with Grey Green, which had been pioneered by Empire's Best. Later in the year, on 25 September, National Travel (East) – which had earlier been renamed from National Travel (North East) – set up a new express coach interchange at its former Sheffield United Tours Charlotte Road, Sheffield, depot that, similarly to Cheltenham, provided a comprehensive link up of services at 2.30 p.m. each day. Prior to this, National Travel (Midlands) was absorbed into National Travel (East) and National Travel (West) under a restructuring, the latter of which had in turn been renamed from National Travel (North West).

Several changes took place in 1978, the most obvious being the application of the National Express fleet name to all National Travel's coaches (this title having only been used on publicity material and timetables since 1974). In addition, Yelloway of Rochdale surrendered its Lancashire to London service to National Travel (West) in return for increased duties on the Lancashire to South West corridor and a share in the Sheffield to Colchester service from 9 September, which was jointly operated with Premier Travel of Cambridge. Under a major reshuffle at the start of the summer timetable on 21 May, a number of National Travel's express services were, somewhat surprisingly, transferred back to NBC's regional bus and coach subsidiaries, with National Travel (West) losing more than twelve of its services to Ribble and Crosville while Greenslades passed its tours activities in the Plymouth and Torbay areas to Western National (Devon General). Then, in what was almost a reverse move, National Travel (South West) took over all the express coach operations of the Bristol Omnibus Co. on 24 September, while National Express (South East) handed over all its UK express services to the local NBC subsidiaries before being discontinued at the end of the year upon the formation of National Travel (London), which was set up to develop a new private hire, excursions and contracts market. And, if this was not enough, National Travel (West) disposed of its Midlands area depots and operations to Midland Red. Although National Express adorned the rear of some of their coaches with fare-promotion adverts, route branding was relatively uncommon, except for the Flightlink and Jetlink services from London to Heathrow, Gatwick and Luton airports.

Although in many ways 1979 proved to be an uneventful year except for a number of service revisions, improvements and new destinations, some further restructuring took place as the months slipped away, including the disbanding of the Central Activities Group and the appointment of executive directors of National Express and National Holidays, whose roles were to oversee their operations. All was set to change the following year, however, with the most serious challenge to Britain's established express coach service network making its presence felt on 6 October 1980 as a consequence of the 1980 Transport Act. This scrapped the express service licensing system, which had been effective since 1930, and replaced it with a free-for-all, which was subject to passengers being carried for a distance of 30 or more miles. Gone were the days when new licence applications could be challenged by other operators and granted or rejected by area traffic commissioners; instead, anyone could gain a licence to operate an express service without the challenge from objectors.

As had been expected, 6 October brought with it a flood of new express coach services and operators, most of whom chose London as their destination. Fares were extremely competitive and right from the start it was obvious that only a minority of these brave (or foolish!) ventures would succeed. In a bold attempt to break National's monopoly, a consortium under the title of 'British Coachways' was formed by Grey Green, Wallace Arnold, Morris Bros of Swansea, Ellerman Beeline, Shearings-Ribblesdale and Parks of Hamilton, who together embarked upon an ambitious programme of routes to London from a number of provincial towns and cities. Soon after its inauguration, and although British Coachways was joined by Barton Transport, Excelsior of Bournemouth, Bristol-based Warner Fairfax and Yorks Travel, Northampton, it was not helped by having to use a barren plot of land with few facilities (formerly a railway goods yard) behind St Pancras railway station as its London terminal. Within weeks a price war commenced between National Express and British Coachways and escalated in December. By January 1981 it was becoming clear that National Express was winning the battle after announcing a staggering 55 per cent increase in the number of journeys undertaken and a massive 53 per cent increase in revenue. By the early summer, competition began to fade and many of the new independent's services had already been discontinued, and Barton Transport, Yorks Travel and Warner Fairfax had all withdrawn from the British Coachways consortium in April, with Grey Green following on 1 July. After a slow death and the withdrawal of Wallace Arnold and Morris Bros, the end came on 18 October 1982 when British Coachways was disbanded, with its only continuing service being that operated by Excelsior between London and Poole. This, unbelievably, survived until November 1998, when it was then sold to National Express.

Despite the battles resulting from the deregulation of express coach services in October 1980, some good was achieved from it and a tiny handful of companies did manage to succeed in their new surroundings. Two of these were Trathens and Glennline, with the former launching a service from Plymouth to London using luxurious double-deck Neoplan Skyliner coaches and the latter running from Exeter to the capital. After Trathens acquired Glennline during the spring of 1981, it joined forces with National Express on 8 November and renamed its non-stop service the 'Rapide Shuttle', on which a smartly dressed stewardess served hot drinks and snacks en route. Prior to this, Whittle's of Highley, who had started some successful services branded 'Goldhawk' that worked from Shropshire and parts of the West Midlands to London in October 1980, merged these with National Express on 5 April 1981, while Wallace Arnold continued their non-stop London to Plymouth and London to Yorkshire services in their own right under the 'Pullman Express' banner from 1 November 1981, upon which free coffee was also served en route by an onboard hostess.

A new innovation from 21 September 1981 was the launch of a parcels service under the title 'National Dispatch' in conjunction with Marlaway Ltd, a London-based specialist parcels pick-up and delivery organisation. Initially, the service was only available between London, Birmingham, Manchester and Liverpool for small parcels, which were collected by Marlaway and taken to the nearest National Express coach station, where they were placed on the first coach to leave for the city they were to be delivered to. They would then be collected by a local company upon arrival for transit to the consignee's address. Then, towards the end of the year, National Express began its new Aircoach services to London's Heathrow and Gatwick airports. These were operated in conjunction with British Airways and ran from Cardiff, Newport and Bristol to Heathrow, and from Bristol, Bournemouth and Southampton to Gatwick. Accordingly, some of the coaches had 'Aircoach' branding added to their livery.

As stated previously, since National Travel had an insufficient number of coaches with which to operate the whole of the National Express network, coaches from a number of NBC regional subsidiaries were also scheduled throughout the year. These were closely vetted to ensure that they met the high standards demanded by National Express and it was not unknown for the occasional inferior vehicle to be refused and returned to its owner without payment, which was made at 1p per seat per mile (i.e. for a forty-nine-seater this would be 49p per mile).

Following the success of the Rapide services between London and the West Country, National Express took the decision to extend this branding to the London–Swansea service from 16 May 1982 and on the London–Manchester service from 20 June. Not initially having enough suitably equipped coaches for these new services, National Express, quite embarrassingly, had to hire some MAN single-deckers from Trathens for the Swansea route, while National Travel (West) refurbished three of its Duple-bodied Leyland Leopards for the route to Manchester. Looking to further expand its new Rapide network, National Express joined forces with Wallace Arnold on 11 July. Wallace Arnold already operated a similar service from Yorkshire to London, and so the two companies merged this into a new jointly operated 'Yorkshire Rapide' service. For National's contribution, a small batch of Duple Goldliner-bodied Dennis Falcon V coaches were ordered (some of which were allocated to West Yorkshire Road Car Co. for operation upon their arrival in August), while Wallace Arnold used two Plaxton-bodied Leyland Leopards and a trio of new Bova Europas.

Despite single-deck coaches having reigned supreme within National Express for several years, the advent of luxurious double-deckers in some independent fleets persuaded National to consider this direction and to this end a prototype was built by Eastern Coach Works on a Leyland Olympian chassis, making its debut on 16 August when it took up its duties on the Bristol to London service. Wearing Wessex fleet names and painted in National Travel's standard white livery, it immediately proved popular with passengers and provoked more thought for the future. Following on from the Marlaway experimental parcels service, National Express joined forces with Britain's largest parcel carrier TNT in September to provide a same-day door-to-door service using the same basic methods as those employed with Marlaway.

1983 witnessed continued improvements to services and new routes being inaugurated, and following the collapse of Magic Bus in December of the previous year, National Express created a new division on 22 May under the title 'Supabus', which was designed to link all the continental services operated by government-approved operators. It initially acted as a marketing agent for twenty services from London to the Continent that were operated by Budget-Bus and Euroways, as well as its own services across the Irish Sea, and considerably widened its experience as far as overseas coach travel was concerned. On the same day, National Express launched its first inter-urban Rapide service from Manchester to Glasgow while a new Cheltenham/Sheffield-style interchange point was set up at Northampton, linking the Midlands and the West Country with East Anglia. Following this, the Sheffield facility was partly superseded by a two-hourly interchange at Digbeth, Birminghm. In addition, in order to adequately cater for the summer peak, a whole range of daytime and overnight journeys were introduced towards the end of June in conjunction with the state-owned Scottish Bus Group between Scotland and some English coastal resorts. Then, as the year rolled on, more inter-urban and London Rapide services were introduced in a bid to speed up journey times by eliminating the need for en route refreshment stops and so on.

A visible change introduced by National Express in 1983 was the introduction of a new corporate livery. While this retained the all-over white, it was enhanced by a series of alternate red and blue 'speed stripes' (resembling a venetian blind), which were applied immediately aft of the front wheel arch. Meanwhile, the NBC relaxed its previously rigid policy relating to its 'local coach' livery to allow its regional subsidiaries to move away from the previous poppy red or leaf green and white, and enabling them to introduce their own schemes. This was immediately welcomed and soon more colourful liveries began to appear across the whole of the country, although all had to be based on the new National Express 'stripy' style. In the metropolis, the NBC set up a new division under the title 'London Crusader', whose purpose was to market the NBC in all its guises in the capital. Since its creation, the new division has evolved a sightseeing package on which a number of open- and closed-top double-deckers have been operated and National Express in London has been promoted. Following its success, similar operations were set up in other parts of the country under the titles 'Birmingham Crusader' and 'Kent Crusader', both of which were entrusted with similar responsibilities. At the same time, in September 1983 the eighty-four individual travel agencies within the NBC were consolidated and given the name 'National Travelworld', and to publicise this several buses operated by NBC regional subsidiaries were given all-over advert liveries similar to those already promoting National Holidays.

Continuing its ever-ongoing restructuring, 1 January 1984 saw the formation of the National Products Group, which took control of National Express, National Holidays, London Crusader, London's Victoria Coach Station, London Country Bus Services Ltd, Birmingham Crusader, Kent Crusader and National Travelworld. At first glance, this seemed like a resurrection of the old Central Activities Group, although the new body had much wider responsibilities including the development of all the area's leisure travel opportunities. Then, on 22 January, the use of St Margaret's coach station, Cheltenham, as an interchange ceased, being replaced by the greater use of other established interchanges at Bristol and Birmingham. Then, another new NBC coaching subsidiary was formed on the following day, when the eighteen-vehicle Pilgrim Coaches was created from Shamrock & Rambler's Southampton operations. At the same time, Midland Red East was renamed Midland Fox.

In addition to the expansion of Rapide services at the start of the 1984 summer timetable, several new routes were inaugurated between English and Scottish towns and cities in conjunction with the Scottish Bus Group, which saw Scottish Citylink coaches travelling to new destinations south of the border and National Express vehicles venturing much further north. Immediately prior to these changes, a new type of double-deck coach – the tri-axle MCW Metroliner – was introduced on 27 April on several National Express Rapide and conventional services, while the single-deck fleet also continued to be upgraded. In addition, the first of twenty-seven Plaxton-bodied Neoplan N722 double-deck coaches also made its debut and, like the Metroliners, these were allocated to various NBC regional subsidiaries. Then, on 20 May, what was perhaps the largest reorganisation since the formation of the National Travel companies took place when their control was transferred to NBC regional bus- and coach-operating subsidiaries such as Ribble and West Riding. Later in the year, National Travel (East) purchased the holiday operations of Leicester-based Neilsons together with its two Jonckheere-bodied Volvo B10Ms on 6 November, maintaining these in their existing liveries for operation on their former owner's holiday tours. Finally,

Supabus expanded its European network with the addition of several new destinations in conjunction with P&O Ferries, Townsend Thoresen, Grey Green and Frank Harris Coaches, while introducing a new winter timetable with more departures.

With the 1985 Transport Act looming and the planned break-up of the National Bus Company on the horizon, it was wondered what the future would hold for National Express, and whether or not it would survive in its present form. In the event, however, it was not until 14 July 1986 that the first effects were seen, when National Holidays was sold to Pleasurama (who had purchased Shearings in 1984), after which the NBC subsidiaries that previously provided coaches no longer did so. Meanwhile, National Express continued in much the same way it had in the past, except that several NBC subsidiaries had been sold to the private sector, although they continued to provide coaches under contract agreements. Then, after continuing without further significant change, the NBC sold its National Travel (East) business together with eighty-four coaches to ATL Holdings Ltd at Sheffield on 29 January 1987, before then selling National Express to its management on 17 March 1988 under the title National Express Holdings Ltd and the National Travelworld travel agency business to Badgerline Holdings a week later, on 24 March. Finally, it sold London's Victoria Coach Station and its headquarters to London Regional Transport on 31 October 1988. On the flipside of the coin, however, National Express purchased Crosville Wales in October and followed this when it bought Euroline, with its London–Paris and Amsterdam services, from Grey Green in December. In addition, it formed a new joint venture company, Durham Travel Services, from United Automobile Services coaching operations, which also took place in October.

Under its new private ownership, National Express soon began to expand and in January 1989 linked up with Thandi Coaches to form Thandi Express – a company catering mainly for Asian coach travellers, although this was unsuccessful and was wound up in July. Following this, it created another joint venture company in April with former Drawlane coach operator Shamrock & Rambler – Dorset Travel Services – and also created London Express, which was a network of feeder services providing twice-daily connections at Victoria Coach Station with the main National Express network. Then, in June, National Express bought the fifty-five-vehicle Merseyside-based Amberline, which it made a subsidiary of Crosville Wales, before purchasing ATL Holdings in July (which included SUT, dealers Carlton PSV and Yelloway-Trathen). Continuing its expansion, and proving 1979 to be a busy year, National Express formed yet another joint venture company from West Yorkshire Road Car Co.'s twenty-one-vehicle coaching operation in July – Yorkshire Voyager Travel Services. A few days after this, on 4 August, when its agreement with Scottish Citylink came to an end, it bought Stagecoach's Scottish coach operations, which it rebranded 'Caledonian Express' and placed under a new company – Tayside Travel Services – with Stagecoach agreeing to allow it to use its name for two years to assist in a smooth transition. In addition, National Express purchased the Euroways services from London to Alicante, Barcelona and Paris from Wallace Arnold in October, thus further expanding its European network. Finally, after selling SUT's bus operations to South Yorkshire PTE subsidiary Hallam Bus Company, its coaching unit at Sheffield was reformed as Rotherham Travel Services. Meanwhile, earlier in the year, National Express had unveiled the Expressliner on 20 March – a new purpose-built coach created by National Express, Plaxton and Volvo to Rapide standard. The coach was exclusively made available on lease to all its contractors through a new company – National Expressliners Ltd, which was formed in conjunction with Plaxton Roadlease. Later specifications for the Expressliner, which was based on Plaxton's Paramount 3500-bodied Volvo B10M, included a non-Rapide version, in which the servery was replaced with three extra seats.

It was not until May 1990 that any further significant events took place. The first was a major attack on Scottish Citylink, when fare cuts and improved timetables were introduced. These led to the launching of a new express service between Glasgow and Edinburgh in September, which it branded 'Merry-go-Round'. In October, London Express was quietly abandoned while Rotherham Travel Services was also closed. Then, in December, National Express divided its Amberline operation and part went to a new subsidiary, Roadmaster Travel Services, which was based in Birmingham.

After selling Yorkshire Voyger Travel Services in March, following which it was immediately closed down, the next milestone in National Express' history came on 23 July 1991 when the Drawlane Transport Group bought a 25 per cent share and a consortium, comprising a number of City investment companies, purchased the remaining 75 per cent of National Express Holdings Ltd. Almost before the ink had dried on its change of ownership, National Express sold its interest in Durham Travel Services to its management in August and then in October purchased Speedlink Airport Services together with its Jetlink brand from Drawlane. Then, just as it was beginning to settle down under its new ownership, the National Express Group was successfully floated on to the stock market via the London Stock Exchange at a share price of 165p on 1 December 1992. Just as the year was ending, a new subsidiary was created under the name Express Travel Services, which took over Roadmaster Travel Services and Tayside Travel Services.

Compared to 1991, the year that followed was comparatively quiet. In April, National Express sold its 50 per cent shareholding in Trathens Travel Services to the Trathens family, while also selling Dorset Travel Services to Bournemouth Transport, thus divesting itself of all its joint operating ventures. Conversely, 1993 proved to be a year of great activity, which started in March when it sold an 80 per cent stake in its Carlton PSV dealership to Stuart Johnson, who renamed the company SJ Carlton. Then, a month later, National Express gave its contractors the freedom to lease coaches other than the Expressliner and allowed them to operate Van Hool-bodied vehicles and Dennis Javelins if they so wished. Following this and continuing to seek expansion, National Express purchased Scottish Citylink in May and sold Express Travel of Perth to British Bus before buying East Midlands Airport in August.

In the meantime, after banning smoking on all its coaches in 1992, part of a further restructuring took place in October 1994 when a newly branded service named Airlinks was introduced specifically for the growing airport market, which was gradually rolled out across various corridors to London Heathrow, Gatwick and Manchester airports. Then, in April 1995, National Express took over Yorkshire Express, against whom it had been competing on services from Bradford and Leeds to London since the autumn of 1993. Following this, Scottish Citylink purchased Highland Country Buses from Rapsons in January 1996, and three months later acquired a minority stake in West Coast Motors. This was followed in September with the purchase of a 25 per cent share in Kyle of Lochalsh-based Skyeways Coaches. Meanwhile, in March 1996, National Express had purchased Flightlink from Birmingham-based Flights, with whom the operation of the services remained. However, after National Express was awarded the railway franchise ScotRail on 31 March 1997, it was instructed by the Mergers and Monopolies Commission to dispose of Scottish Citylink and to this end it sold Highlands Country Buses back to Rapsons in August 1998. At the same time, it sold Citylink to ComfortDelGro, who were the owners of Metroline in London. Unfortunately, when the ScotRail franchise expired on 16 October 2004, National Express failed to regain it and it passed to FirstGroup. Prior to this, National Express Group had expanded its portfolio with the purchase of Birmingham-based West Midlands Travel from its management owners in April 1995 and Dundee-based Tayside Public Transport in February 1997; although, as neither of these were coach operators, no further mention of them will be made within these pages. Then, on 1 January 1999, a new company was formed called Airlinks The Airport Coach Company Ltd, whose aim was to expand its focus on airport-scheduled and contract bus and coach services (which were painted in liveries such as Flightlink, Speedlink and Jetlink). To further consolidate this, the third-party interests in the Jetlink brand were purchased, which were followed in June 1999 by Heathrow-based Silverwing Transport Services with eighty-eight vehicles and Cambridge Coach Services from Blazefield Holdings with twenty-two coaches in October 1999. This made Airlinks the largest operator of both scheduled and contract services to BAA and airline operators.

After all these restructurings within National Express, a period of calm prevailed, and it was not until the twenty-first century had been entered that any more significant changes occurred. Continuing its expansions in regard to airport operations, Airlinks purchased London United's Airbus service, together with nineteen Volvo Olympians in January 2000, as well as Skills of Nottingham's Brighton operation along with eight coaches. This was followed by the acquisition of Tellings Golden Miller-owned Capital Logistics with seventy-one vehicles in April 2000. Then, towards the end of the year, the onboard catering facilities (which had gradually been withdrawn from Rapide services in the latter years of the 1990s) were removed completely due to decreasing demand, thus bringing to an end a service that had been available for over forty years.

Although the corporate National Express livery had remained largely unchanged for more than twenty years, it was decided in 2003 that it needed to be updated. As such, a new version was launched on 3 March. This had its fleet name applied in lower case lettering with a capital 'N' and 'E' – with 'National' being in blue and 'Express' in red – and featured two large, solid circles aft of the rear wheel arch (again, one red and the other blue), incorporating a white arrow aimed from one to the other. This was quickly applied to all of the coaches operating on National Express services and was also added to all publicity material. A year earlier, National Express had launched another new generation of its Plaxton-bodied Expressliner coach, which, to appease operators, offered more choice in some of its mechanical features, while also being available with a wheelchair lift. Then, in 2006, the Caetano Levante made its debut. Based on a Volvo B12B chassis, this had been developed specially for National Express and was exclusively for the use of its own fleet and those of its contracted operators. One of its special features was the 'magic floor' that was fitted into its front passenger entrance door, which could lift wheelchairs into a dedicated area at the front of the coach. From 2007 the Levante was also available on the Scania K340 chassis in both two- and three-axle configuration. At around the same time, National Express modified its livery yet again and, although retaining its corporate white base colour, its fleet name was applied in all-lower-case lettering ('national' in blue, 'express' in red) while its solid red and blue circles aft of the rear axle of its coaches were replaced with diagonal grey bars.

Continuing to seek expansion, National Express further consolidated its position as the country's largest coach operator when in April 2007 it joined forces with London-based Hotelink to form National Express Dot2Dot to provide an on-demand airport shuttle transfer service from central London hotels to Heathrow and Gatwick airports. For this new role it used a fleet of sixty luxurious Mercedes-Benz minibuses, but it sadly never reached its potential and was sold to Corot of Milton Keynes in November 2009. As the search for expansion continued unabated, National Express purchased the seventy-five-vehicle, Gillingham-based Kings Ferry Travel Group in November 2007, which specialised in commuter coach travel and private hire and traded under Kings Ferry and Travel Link identities. On this occasion, however, rather than repaint its acquired coaches in corporate National Express livery, they retained their autonomy, existing colours and fleet names. A further development in 2007 saw National Express entering into an agreement with Wembley Stadium (London) to be its official travel provider, and to this end the Wembley logo was added to all of its coaches. Although route branding had never been a major feature of National Express, except for the London airport routes, the company was always happy to promote special events, such as Armed Forces Day, the Commonwealth Games and Olympic successes by partly or fully wrapping one or two of its coaches in commemorative liveries. In addition, from 6–12 June 2016, Kings Ferry reprogrammed the electronic destination display of all its coaches to read 'Happy Birthday Ma'am' and the fleet-name lettering of one to read 'Queens Ferry' to mark the 90th birthday of HM Queen Elizabeth II.

In April 2011, National Express began 24/7 operations on its Dover to London service. During the following year it rolled this out to a number of other routes too, which was followed by the introduction of Wi-Fi on its Stansted to London service on 9 June in a move that was gradually extended to all of its coaches throughout the UK. Looking to expand its airport coach market, National Express linked up with Ryanair in May 2013 in a deal that enabled passengers to book airport coach transfers at the same time as booking their flight, as well as on board every Ryanair aircraft. Finding this to be successful, a similar arrangement was made with Wizz Air in February of the following year and also with easyJet. Meanwhile, National Express had struck a deal with the Post Office in October 2013, under which coach tickets could be purchased at any of its branches throughout the UK.

Continuing to add to its ever-growing portfolio, on 16 December 2016 National Express purchased the seventy-coach commuter coach and private hire operator Clarkes of London. Although it retained its own livery and identity, and continued to operate from its depots at Lower Sydenham (London) and Hoo (Rochester), its management was transferred to Kings Ferry.

Today, National Express maintains a highly standardised fleet of coaches on 135 services across the UK, and after more than two decades has reintroduced double-deckers in a bid to enhance capacity where needed. Although it provides vehicles from its own fleet, it still largely relies on around forty independent operators who each supply coaches under contract to strictly controlled specifications. While all of these are painted in corporate National Express livery, at busy times this edict is relaxed to allow coaches in their owners' colours to be used, thus providing a touch of variety on such occasions.

Finally, for those who like statistics, in 2016 National Express undertook 19 million passenger journeys, served over 900 destinations across the UK, provided 24-hour services to all of the UK's major airports, generated £282.8 million revenue and enjoyed a £33.3 million profit. Who can argue with that?

Two Southdown Harrington-bodied Leyland Leopards rest between duties – 1720 (2720 CD) still in its owner's pre-NBC livery with 1757 (BUF 157C) having succumbed to corporate National white. (F. W. York)

Specially built in 1974 for use as a mobile conference centre, National Travel South East Leyland National JMY 120N is seen here after being preserved and restored to its former glory. (K. A. Jenkinson)

Painted in corporate National livery and with a 'not licensed' label in its windscreen is Southern Vectis Plaxton-bodied Bedford VAL70 411 (SDL 744J), an uncommon model for the NBC. (F. W. York)

Employed on National Express services between North West England and London was Standerwick ECW-bodied Bristol VRLLH6L 79 (PRN 79K), which is seen here in 1977. (T. W. W. Knowles)

Seen in Portsmouth on its way to Bournemouth in 1977 is National-liveried East Kent Willowbrook-bodied AEC Reliance OJG 134F. (F. W. York)

With coach seats fitted to an ECW bus shell, Lincolnshire Road Car Co. Bristol RELH6G 1435 (LFE 144H) is seen here painted in corporate National coaching livery. (P. T. Stokes)

Displaying a Tillings fleet name, Duple (Northern)-bodied Bristol RESH6G (YTW 540F) began life in 1968 with Eastern National. (K. A. Jenkinson collection)

Seen at the British Coach Rally at Brighton in 1977 is National Travel (South East) left-hand drive Willowbrook-bodied AEC Reliance OYT 530R. (K. A. Jenkinson collection)

Displaying Mansfield District and East Midland fleet names, Duple-bodied Leyland Leopard C4 (NNN 4M) is pictured in Portsmouth undertaking a private hire duty in 1979. (F. W. York)

On hire to London Transport for operation on its sightseeing tour, National Travel (South East) Willowbrook-bodied Bedford YRT JMY 121N is seen collecting its passengers at Grosvenor Gardens, Victoria. (T. W. W. Knowles)

Above: Parked at Southdown's Hilsea depot in February 1979 are Western National Plaxton-bodied Bristol RELH6G 2395 (UTT 564J) with Royal Blue fleet name and Black & White Plaxton-bodied Leyland Leopard 326 (YDF 326K), both of which are painted in corporate National livery. (F. W. York)

Left: Displayed at the 1979 British Coach Rally at Brighton carrying Frames branding is National Travel (East) Duple-bodied Leyland Leopard BWE 203T. (T. W. W. Knowles)

Arriving at Bradford Interchange at the end of the first British Coachways journey from London on 6 October 1980 is Grey Green Duple-bodied Leyland Leopard YYL 772T. (K. A. Jenkinson)

Seen after being preserved and painted in British Coachways livery is ex-Morris Bros, Swansea, Plaxton-bodied Volvo B58 FTH 991W. (K. A. Jenkinson collection)

Painted in Townsend Thoresen Holidays livery in June 1981 is Southdown Plaxton-bodied Leyland Leopard 1267 (K. A. Jenkinson)

Resting on Hayling Island in 1981 and painted in P&O Landtours livery for its National contracted duties is Shamrock & Rambler Plaxton-bodied Leyland Leopard 3072 (ELJ 210V). (F. W. York)

Adorned in National's corporate white livery is United Counties ECW-bodied Bristol RELH6G 269 (KRP 269E), which was new in 1967. (K. A. Jenkinson)

Pictured in Plymouth in 1981 with a Western National slipboard covering its Royal Blue fleet name is National corporate liveried Plaxton-bodied Leyland Leopard 3518 (VOD 618S). (K. A. Jenkinson)

Resting at Portsmouth in 1982 are Oxford South Midland Duple (Northern)-bodied Bristol LH6L 32 (UMO 688G) and Southdown Plaxton-bodied Leyland Leopard 1233 (LCD 233F). (F. W. York)

Leaving Victoria Coach Station, London, is Trathens of Yelverton's Neoplan Skyliner STT 602X, which carries West Country London Rapide and National Express lettering, as well as its owner's identity. (K. A. Jenkinson)

Wearing National Travel London fleet names in 1982 is Plaxton-bodied Leyland Tiger SMY 629X. (K. A. Jenkinson)

Displaying National Holidays fleet names is Southern Vectis Duple-bodied Bedford YMT 303 (TDL 303S) (K. A. Jenkinson collection)

Caught by the camera at Victoria, London, in 1983 is Cumberland ECW-bodied Leyland Leopard 639 (VAO 639Y) in corporate National livery. (K. A. Jenkinson)

Seen at Blackpool in August 1983 displaying National Travel East as its only identity, all-white-liveried Plaxton 3500-bodied Leyland Tiger WWA 303Y shows Club 18–30 Holidays in its upper windscreen. On its left is a National Holidays-liveried Leyland Leopard, while on its right is National Travel East Plaxton-bodied Leyland Leopard YWE 509M with National Express lettering. (K. A. Jenkinson)

Awaiting its inbound ferry passengers at the Isle of Man sea terminal at Liverpool in July 1983 is National Travel West's ECW-bodied Leyland Leopard 93 (ANA 93 Y). (K. A. Jenkinson)

Shamrock & Rambler Duple-bodied Leyland Leopard 3080 (RUF 811H), seen here in National Express corporate livery, started life with Southdown in 1970. (F. W. York)

Painted in London Crusader livery and operated on sightseeing tours from Trafalgar Square, London, is London Country open-top Park Royal-bodied Leyland Atlantean AN5 (JPL 105K). (T. W. W. Knowles)

Displayed at the 30th British Coach Rally at Brighton in 1984, National Travel (East) Jonckheere-bodied Volvo B10M A335 YDT wore a dedicated livery for operation on behalf of Intasun Tours. (T. W. W. Knowles)

Awaiting its passengers at Portsmouth in June 1984 and wearing National Express 'venetian blind' livery is Pilgrim Coaches Plaxton-bodied Leyland Leopard NEL 115P, which began life with Hants & Dorset. (K. A. Jenkinson)

Standing at its express service terminus on Pancras Road, London, on 14 June 1984, while operating independent of National Express, is Excelsior's Plaxton-bodied Neoplan N122 XEL 24. (K. A. Jenkinson)

National Express promoted its fares and services with adverts on numerous National Bus Company subsidiary's buses, as illustrated here on West Yorkshire Road Car Co. ECW-bodied Bristol VRT 1973 (RWT 548R). (John Bentley)

Seen at Bridlington in June 1985 painted in a dedicated livery for Club 18–30 is National Travel East Jonckheere-bodied Volvo B10M A310 XHE. (K. A. Jenkinson)

Smith of Reading's Caetano-bodied Toyota BB30R B105 YUC in Swan National livery stands outside the Queen's Building at Heathrow Airport, London in 1985. (T. W. W. Knowles)

Performing car park shuttle duties at the NEC, Birmingham, Midland Red North Plaxton Paramount 3500-bodied Leyland Tiger 1512 (A512 HVT) carries National Express Rapide and Chaserider identities. (K. A. Jenkinson)

Standing on Ecclestone Bridge, London, in April 1986 while painted in Insight International livery is London Country Berkhof-bodied Leyland Tiger BTL24 (B124 KPF). (K. A. Jenkinson)

Another of London Country's Berkhof-bodied Leyland Tigers, BTL25 (B125 KPF), is seen here at Epsom Downs on a private hire to the Derby race meeting while wearing National Holidays livery. (T. W. W. Knowles)

Sporting a National Travel identifier above its front wheel arch, National Travel East's Plaxton-bodied Leyland Leopard JWE 246W is seen here outside Blackpool's Coliseum coach station on 26 June 1986. (K. A. Jenkinson)

With a 'Tourist Trail' logo alongside its Yelloway fleet name, Plaxton-bodied Volvo B10M XWK 7X leaves Victoria Coach Station, London, on a National Express journey to York on 14 July 1986. (K. A. Jenkinson)

Painted in Travelscene livery, National London Bova Futura A667 EMY heads along Elizabeth Bridge, London, on 14 July 1986. (K. A. Jenkinson)

National Express contractor Kingston of Yeovil's corporate-liveried Duple-bodied Bedford YNV C175 HYD rests at its owner's depot in May 1986. (F. W. York)

National Travel East Duple Caribbean-bodied Volvo B10M THL 294Y displays its National Holidays logo as it leaves Bradford Transport Interchange. (K. A. Jenkinson)

Ambassador Travel MCW Metroliner 915 (C915 BPW) is pictured here outside Victoria Coach Station, London. (T. W. W. Knowles)

In 1986, Percivals of Oxford added National Express logos to its Plaxton-bodied Leyland Leopard 80 (VWL 96, originally LWL 744W) when it joined the list of contractors. (K. A. Jenkinson collection)

Seen outside Victoria Coach Station, London, while painted in corporate National Express 'venetian blind' livery is Trent Willowbrook-bodied Leyland Leopard 155 (VNN 55Y). (T. W. W. Knowles)

Resting within the confines of Gatwick Airport in April 1987 is Swan National VW minibus C435 SRX. (K. A. Jenkinson)

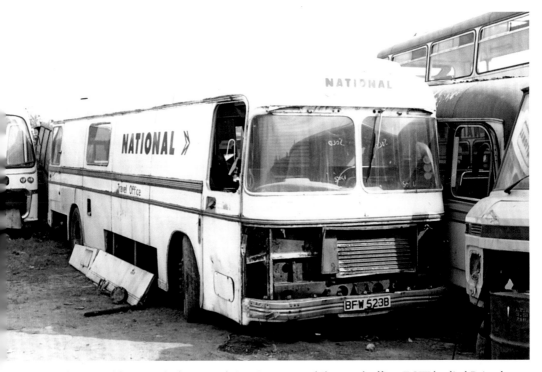

Having been used by Lincolnshire Road Car Co. as a mobile travel office, ECW-bodied Bristol RELH6G 1404 (BFW 532B, originally registered WVL 515) awaits its fate at dealer W. North's Sherburn-in-Elmet yard in 1987. (K. A. Jenkinson collection)

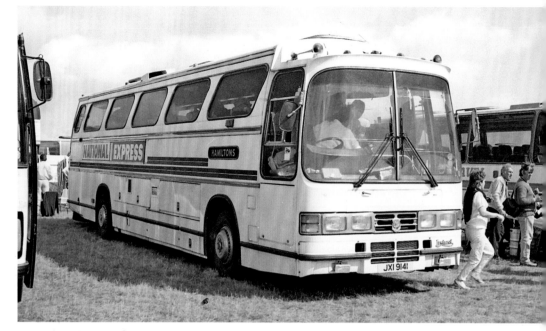

Painted in National Express livery and seen here at the Derby on Epsom Downs is Hamiltons of Uxbridge's Duple Goldliner III-bodied Leyland Tiger JXI 9141 (originally BLH 717Y). (T. W. W. Knowles)

Parked at the Cambridge depot of its owner Premier Travel on 27 April 1987 and wearing National Express corporate livery is Plaxton Paramount 3200-bodied Leyland Tiger 299 (FAV 566Y). (K. A. Jenkinson)

Painted in National Travel Euro-Sleeper Coach livery, National Travel (East) Jonckheere-bodied Volvo B10M A312 XHE leaves Buchanan bus station, Glasgow on 9 May 1987 on a National Express Yelloway duty. (K. A. Jenkinson)

Wearing National Express corporate livery and seen here in Brighton is Plaxton Viewmaster-bodied Leyland Leopard JTM 104V of National Express contractor Sonner of Gillingham, who traded as Scorpion Tours. (T. W. W. Knowles)

Seen on the parking area behind Crossfield bus station, Halifax, on 26 April 1988 wearing National Express corporate livery is Limebourne of London's Duple 320-bodied Leyland Tiger D133 HML. (K. A. Jenkinson)

National Travel (London) Berkhof-bodied DAF SB2300 A648 NOO, painted in Hoverspeed livery, enjoys the sunshine at the Epsom Derby while undertaking a private hire duty. (T. W. W. Knowles)

Sporting National Holidays livery, United's Bova Europa 1150 (B330 ANY) squeezes through Harrogate bus station in 1988. (K. A. Jenkinson collection)

Used as a lounge at Victoria Coach Station, London, for National Express' Birmingham Shuttle passengers is Roe-bodied Leyland Atlantean DUA 471K, which began life with Leeds City Transport in 1971. (K. A. Jenkinson collection)

An unusual vehicle to wear corporate National Express livery is Crosville Wales Caetano-bodied Iveco 49.10 MCF 277 (F77 CJC), which is seen here in Shrewsbury in August 1989. (K. A. Jenkinson collection)

Freshly repainted with both Caledonian Express and Stagecoach fleet names and seen here at Walnut Grove, Perth, depot on 27 October 1989 is ex-Stagecoach Neoplan Jetliner 4585 SC, which was originally registered A216 LWD. (S. A. Jenkinson)

Also displaying Caledonian Express fleet names together with Rapide branding, former Stagecoach Neoplan Skyliner E92 VWA leaves Kirkcaldy bus station on a journey to Ayr. (K. A. Jenkinson)

Painted in National Express Rapide livery is Yelloway Neoplan Jetliner TWG 561Y. (T. W. W. Knowles)

Passing through Stockport bus station on its way to London on 3 October 1989 is former SUT's Neoplan Skyliner OES 628Y, which began life registered MVL 608Y with Stagecoach at Perth. (K. A. Jenkinson)

Displaying London Express fleet names is Reeve Burgess-bodied Leyland Swift 144 (G341 VHU). (F. W. York)

Heading northbound to Newcastle-upon-Tyne at speed along an almost deserted M1 motorway in May 1990 is an unidentified United MCW Metroliner. (F. W. York)

Adorned with Heathrow Flightline branding, London Country Berkhof-bodied Leyland Tiger BTL39 (C139 SPB) enters Victoria Coach Station, London, in October 1990. (K. A. Jenkinson)

New to National Travel London, Plaxton-bodied Leyland Tiger SMY 636X is seen here in October 1990 at Cardiff bus station after its sale to contractor Yardleys of Birmingham. It is seen wearing National Express livery. (K. A. Jenkinson)

Owned by National Express contractor Dack of Terrington St Clement, Plaxton Paramount 3200-bodied Leyland Tiger B387 UEX has just arrived at Victoria Coach Station, London, in September 1990. (K. A. Jenkinson)

Standing outside Wellington Street coach station, Leeds, is Midland United Transport's National Express-liveried ex-Yelloway Plaxton Supreme-bodied AEC Reliance SBU 303R. (K. A. Jenkinson)

United's National Express Rapide-liveried MCW Metroliner 154 (A113 KBA) passes London Express-branded Plaxton-bodied Leyland Tiger TPL91 (B291 KPF) on Buckingham Palace Road, London, in April 1990. (K. A. Jenkinson)

Wearing full National Express corporate livery, Galloway of Mendlesham's Plaxton-bodied DAF SB2305 F886 SRT arrives at Victoria Coach Station at the end of its journey from Hadleigh in October 1990. (K. A. Jenkinson)

Dorset Travel Services Plaxton-bodied Leyland Tiger STL3 (C203 PPE) stands in Buckingham Palace Road outside Victoria Coach Station, London, in April 1990, having just completed a National Express Rapide journey from Weymouth. (K. A. Jenkinson)

Once a member of the British Coachways consortium but now a National Express contractor, Barton of Chilwell's Plaxton Paramount 3200-bodied DAF MB230 1645 (E645 DAU) heads along Buckingham Palace Road, London, in May 1990. (K. A. Jenkinson)

Wearing a promotional livery for National Holidays, and seen here near Haworth, is West Yorkshire Road Car Co. ECW-bodied Bristol VRT 1765 (SUB 789W). (F. W. York)

Seen in Victoria Coach Station, London, in April 1990 is Yorkshire Voyager National Express Rapide-liveried Plaxton-bodied Neoplan N722 C752 CWX, which was new to West Yorkshire Road Car Co. (K. A. Jenkinson)

National Express contractor Limebourne of London's Van Hool-bodied Volvo B10M F887 SMU enters Victoria Coach Station, London, in April 1990, ready to take up a duty to York. (K. A. Jenkinson)

Another National Express contractor was Chartercoach of Great Ockley, whose Duple 340-bodied Leyland Tiger F132 UMD is seen resting in Victoria Coach Station, London, in September 1990. (K. A. Jenkinson)

Awaiting its Bristol-bound passengers at Portsmouth in 1990 is Wessex MCW Metroliner 131 (C131 CFB). (F. W. York)

Displaying a Cotswold fleet name, Cheltenham & Gloucester Plaxton Paramount 3200-bodied Leyland Tiger 2200 (A200 RHT) collects its Edinburgh-bound passengers in Wellington Street coach station, Leeds. (K. A. Jenkinson)

Painted in corporate National Express Rapide livery and displaying a Cornwall Coaches fleet identifier, Western National 2229 (C975 GCV), a Duple 340-bodied Leyland Tiger, stands in Wellington Street coach station, Leeds, ready to depart to Newcastle-upon-Tyne. (K. A. Jenkinson)

National Express contractor Bleanch of Hetton-le-Hole's ex-Yelloways Plaxton Supreme III-bodied AEC Reliance, WDK 561T, is seen here in Wellington Street coach station, Leeds, with a National Express label at the bottom of its nearside windscreen. It is operating the 325 service from Newcastle-upon-Tyne to Brighton. (K. A. Jenkinson)

Displaying a National fleet name and West Yorkshire identifier on its 'venetian blind' livery, Plaxton-bodied Leyland Leopard 2581 (KUB 555V) stands in Bradford Transport Interchange while operating a local bus duty to Leeds. (K. A. Jenkinson)

With a Northern Rose identifier on its National Express corporate livery, West Yorkshire Road Car Co. ECW-bodied Leyland Leopard 2613 (UWY 88X) rests between duties in Harrogate bus station. (K. A. Jenkinson)

Painted in Caledonian Express livery with Merry-go-Round and Glasgow to Edinburgh branding, Nationwide of Carnwath's Van Hool-bodied DAF 9712 WX is seen here in Buchanan bus station, Glasgow, in 1990. (Campbell Morrison)

Wearing an anonymous white livery and preparing to enter Victoria Coach Station, London, in October 1990 is National Express contractor Kennet & Avon's Berkhof-bodied Volvo B10M BDV 862Y, which began life with Trathens. (K. A. Jenkinson)

New to Southdown registered as A806 CCD, Duple Laser-bodied Leyland Tiger 1006 (A474 NJK) is seen here in corporate National Express 'venetian blind' livery in March 1991. (K. A. Jenkinson)

Pictured in the capital in March 1991 displaying London Express fleet names is London Country Berkhof-bodied Leyland Tiger BTL10 (B110 KPF). (K. A. Jenkinson)

With Supabus lettering in its upper windscreen and Eurobus fleet name, Evans of Penrhyncoch's Plaxton Paramount 3500-bodied Leyland Tiger H179 EJU is seen here at Victoria Coach Station, London, in March 1991. (K. A. Jenkinson)

West Yorkshire Road Car Co. Duple Goldliner-bodied Dennis Falcon V 2202 (TWE 81Y), which was new to Yorkshire Traction, is seen here in York painted in National Express corporate livery. (K. A. Jenkinson)

Roadmaster Travel (National Express) Plaxton Paramount 3500-bodied RTS 9003 (NXI 9003) rests at London Heathrow Airport in July 1991. (K. A. Jenkinson)

New to Cotters, Glasgow, Van Hool-bodied Volvo B10M XHR 104 is seen here in Cardiff bus station in July 1991 while being operated by Byron Coaches, Llansamlet, on a National Express duty to London. (K. A. Jenkinson)

KMP Llanberis Plaxton Paramount 3500-bodied Leyland Tiger 772 URB (which began life with PMT, registered as B30 OBF) with additional Supabus and Bus Eireann fleet names leaves Victoria Coach Station, London, on the first leg of its journey to Dublin. (K. A. Jenkinson)

National Express contractor D-Way Travel of Bungay's MAN SR280 B531 GNV rests in Victoria Coach Station, London, in October 1991. (K. A. Jenkinson)

Galloway of Mendlesham's Plaxton Supreme IV-bodied Bedford YMT BBA 53A (originally KBH 850V) heads past Victoria railway station, London, near the end of its National Express route-081 journey from Great Yarmouth in September 1991. (K. A. Jenkinson)

Wearing a dedicated livery, Speedlink Airport Services Plaxton Paramount 3500-bodied Volvo B10M VII (G811 BPG) arrives at London's Heathrow Airport at the end of its journey from Gatwick in July 1991. (K. A. Jenkinson)

Sporting Midland Red coaches identity on its National Express corporate livery, Midland Red West Plaxton Paramount 3500-bodied Volvo B10M 1001 (FEH 1Y) is seen here in Bradford Transport Interchange. (K. A. Jenkinson)

Passing through City Square, Leeds, in 1991 is National Express contractor AJC Coaches' Duple Caribbean-bodied DAF SB2300 D241L NW, which is in National Express Rapide livery. (K. A. Jenkinson)

Resting outside Victoria Coach Station, London, in October 1992 is contractor Ridgeons Jonckheere-bodied Volvo B10M KIW 7812, which began life with National Travel East registered as A339 YDT. (K. A. Jenkinson)

Arriving at Victoria Coach Station, London, in August 1992 is Bebb, Llantwit Fardre's National Express liveried Setra S215HD J76 VTG. (K. A. Jenkinson)

National Express contractor Shaw Hadwin of Silverdale's Jonckheere-bodied Volvo B10M 118 899 CAN (originally A539 BEC) in National Express Rapide livery passes through Preston bus station in November 1992. (K. A. Jenkinson)

Seen in Victoria Coach Station, London, in August 1992 while undertaking a Shearings National feeder service is Tates of Potton End's Plaxton-bodied Ford R1115 VLV 815 (originally C422 BCR). (K. A. Jenkinson)

SUT (National Express) Sheffield's Neoplan Jetliner D808 RKY rests in Bradford Transport Interchange after completing a Rapide journey from London. (K. A. Jenkinson)

About to leave Victoria Coach Station, London, is Bennett of Uxbridge's Eurolines-liveried TAZ D2300, G715 VRY. (K. A. Jenkinson)

Displaying Eurolines lettering in its upper windscreen, Dorset Travel Services Plaxton Expressliner Mk III-bodied Volvo B10M, PJI 3354 (originally H818 AHS), swings into Basingstoke bus station on 20 February 1993. (F. W. York)

Wessex Duple 340-bodied Leyland Tiger 133 (NAT 860A, originally C133 CFB) arrives at Gloucester bus station en route to Brixham in August 1993. (K. A. Jenkinson)

National Express contractor Shaw Hadwin of Silverdale's Jonckheere-bodied XDG 32 (originally A538 BAC) is seen here in Victoria Coach Station, London, with a 'Merry Christmas' streamer at the top of its windscreen. (K. A. Jenkinson)

Entering Preston bus station in October 1993 is Meddings & Jones, Birmingham's National Express-liveried Leyland Royal Tiger Doyen, D768 POJ. (K. A. Jenkinson)

Western National's National Express Rapide liveried Duple 425 2241 (E207 BOD) stands at Portsmouth Harbour in July 1994. (K. A. Jenkinson)

Peeping out of Stagecoach Western Scottish's Cumnock depot on 3 September 1994 is Citylink-liveried Plaxton Paramount 3500-bodied Volvo B10M CN142 (VLT 272 originally B202 CGA). (K. A. Jenkinson)

Contracted to National Express, Hamilton of Uxbridge's Sanos S315 J602 LLK circumnavigates Marble Arch, London, while on its way to Birmingham in April 1994. (K. A. Jenkinson)

Trathens Travel Services Van Hool Astrobel-bodied Volvo B12 L976 KDT arrives at Preston bus station en route to Blackpool in October 1994. (K. A. Jenkinson)

Arriving at Preston bus station in October 1994 is Stagecoach Western Scottish Citylink-liveried Plaxton 425 SH 108 (J8 WSB). (K. A. Jenkinson)

Dorset Travel Services' corporate National Express-liveried Berkhof-bodied MAN 16.290 331 (L331 BFX) is seen outside London's Victoria Coach Station in February 1995. (K. A. Jenkinson)

A week before being taken over by National Express, Yorkshire Travel's Caetano-bodied DAF SB3000 G952 VBC leaves Victoria Coach Station, London, at the start of its journey to Leeds. (K. A. Jenkinson)

Displaying a National Express logo, former London United Alexander-bodied Volvo Olympian N112 UHP heads to London's Heathrow Airport in September 1995. (K. A. Jenkinson collection)

Seen at Manchester Airport wearing Flightlink livery in October 1995 is Flights of Birmingham's Bova Futura M2 0FTG. (K. A. Jenkinson)

Resting at their Cambridge depot on 14 April 1996 are two Premier Travel Plaxton-bodied Volvo B10Ms – 428 (K458 PNR) with Travelsphere lettering below its windscreen and Eurolines-liveried 437 (J702 CWT). (K. A. Jenkinson)

With 'Express Shuttle Cambridge to London' lettering on its side panels, Premier Travel Services corporate National Express-liveried Plaxton-bodied Volvo B10M 451 (N451 XVA) collects its passengers at Drummer Street bus station, Cambridge, on 14 April 1996. (K. A. Jenkinson)

Displaying 'Rapide Airlink' lettering in its upper windscreen, Wessex Plaxton Expressliner-bodied Volvo B10M 158 (J204 HWS) is seen at its owner's Bristol depot on 13 April 1997. (K. A. Jenkinson)

Painted in Scottish Citylink livery and seen at Buchanan bus station, Glasgow, in February 1997 on a Citylink/National Express journey to Aberdeen is First Aberdeen subsidiary G.E. Mair's Jonckheere-bodied Volvo B10M 706 (FSU 333), which was originally registered G845 GNV. (K. A. Jenkinson)

Passing through Stockport on a National Express journey to Manchester on 3 October 1989 is Amberline-liveried Neoplan Skyliner C792 PEM. (K. A. Jenkinson)

Bebb, Llantwit Fardre's National Express-liveried Setra S250 R35 AWD is seen at Victoria, London, after completing a journey from Cardiff. (K. A. Jenkinson collection)

Collecting its London-bound passengers in Rougier Street, York, is Durham Travel Services Van Hool-bodied Scania K113CRB L3 DTS. (K. A. Jenkinson)

Collecting its passengers at Luton airport on 27 May 1999 and wearing Jetlink branding is Speedlink Airport Services Plaxton-bodied Volvo B10M M724 KPD. (K. A. Jenkinson)

Leaving Meadowhall bus station, Sheffield, en route to Luton is Northumbria's Bova Futura 140 (M122 UUB). (K. A. Jenkinson)

Sporting GoByCoach.com logos on its corporate National Express livery and seen in Bradford on 12 August 2000 is Bebbs, Llantwit Fardre's Plaxton Expressliner-bodied Volvo B10M S47 UBO. (K. A. Jenkinson)

Western National Plaxton-bodied Volvo B10M 2316 (T316 KCV), seen here at Fareham on 29 December 2000, is adorned with graphics to promote 'McDonald's Our Town Story' at the Millennium Dome, London. (F. W. York)

Seen demonstrating its wheelchair lift in October 2002 is First Bristol National Express-liveried Plaxton-bodied Volvo B12M WVo 2EUT. (K. A. Jenkinson)

Tellings Golden Miller Plaxton Premier-bodied Volvo B10M T10 TGM carries a boased at the bottom of its nearside windscreen indicating that it is operating National Express service 300 to Bristol. (F. W. York)

Painted in corporate livery together with Express Shuttle and Leeds to Liverpool route branding, Selwyn of Runcorn's Van Hool-bodied DAF SB4000 103 (TJI 6925 originally YJo 3PPY) is seen here at its owner's depot in April 2003. (K. A. Jenkinson)

Wearing Eurolines and National Express logos is Ulsterbus Plaxton-bodied Volvo B12B 123 (KEZ 9123) seen here en route from Dover to London. (K. A. Jenkinson collection)

Painted in Virgin livery for the Heathrow to Watford Junction Air Link service is National Express Caetano-bodied Volvo B12B NXVC1 (FH05 URN). (K. A. Jenkinson collection)

National Express temporarily converted its Irizar-bodied Scania K114EB4 NXL32 (YN55 NDZ) into a mobile studio for Channel 4's *Big Brother* television programme. Here it is seen in January 2006 undertaking this role. (K. A. Jenkinson collection)

Approaching Meadowhall, Sheffield, on its way to Bradford is Birmingham Coach Company Van Hool-bodied Scania K124IB4 X422 WVO, which has a Shuttle logo added to its National Express fleet name. (K. A. Jenkinson)

Seen at Heathrow Airport wearing Woking Railair branding is National Express Transbus-bodied Volvo B12M NXVP3. (Richard Walter)

Void of its fleet name but using the St George's flag as its livery is National Express Caetano Levante-bodied Volvo B12B CO67 (FH06 EAX), which is seen here at Luton Airport. (K. A. Jenkinson collection)

Leaving Meadowhall bus station, Sheffield, is Nottingham-based Dunn Line's Caetano-bodied Volvo B12B 0626 (FN06 FKZ), which is seen wearing National Express livery with an additional 'Airport' logo. (K. A. Jenkinson)

Operating a National Express service, Excelsior of Bournemouth Plaxton-bodied Volvo B12M 613 (YN05 VSL) is seen here at Hilsea on 10 January 2008. (F. W. York)

Unusually displaying its fleet name in green alongside a shamrock emblem is National Express Irizar-bodied Scania K114EB4 NXL15 (YN05 WJA). (Malcolm Crowe)

National Express contractor Silverdale of Nottingham's Plaxton Elite-bodied Volvo B12B FJ55 DYW is seen leaving Broadmarsh bus station, Nottingham, on a journey to London in April 2008. (K. A. Jenkinson)

Adorned with National Express Dot2Dot logos is Hotelink's silver-liveried VW minibus, YN07NVX. (K. A. Jenkinson)

Posing for the camera when new in September 2008 is Bruce of Salsburgh's Caetano-bodied Scania K348EB6 FJ58 AKK, which, in addition to wearing corporate National Express livery, displays the Scottish saltire on its rear panels. (Scania)

Transferred from The Kings Ferry to National Express and repainted into corporate livery, Hispano Vita-bodied Mercedes-Benz 0404 CO97 (A14T KF originally V899LOH) is seen here at Poole Valley, Brighton, on 17 July 2010. (D. W. Rhodes)

Looking immaculate when caught by the camera at Bean, Kent on 6 August 2010 is The Kings Ferry's Setra S416GT 6.1 (BV55 FPL). (D. W. Rhodes)

Armchair of London's National Express liveried Van Hool-bodied DAF SB4000 YJ04 HHZ looks immaculate as it heads through Chelmsford en route to Liverpool on 21 August 2010. (D. W. Rhodes)

Wearing logos to support Armed Forces Day is Lucketts of Fareham's National Express-liveried Caetano Levante-bodied Scania K340EB4 X4966 (FJ59 APF). (F. W. York)

Sporting Travel Link fleet names, The Kings Ferry's Van Hool-bodied Scania E941B A16 TKF (originally V998 JKK) is seen here on Parrock Street, Gravesend, on 7 April 2011. (D.W. Rhodes)

Painted in a silver livery with VIP lettering is The Kings Ferry Irizar-bodied Scania K124EB V5 PKF, which was originally registered YN54 AKF. (K. A. Jenkinson collection)

Painted in corporate National Express livery, Ulsterbus Plaxton-bodied Volvo B12B 122 (KEZ 9122), seen here in Belfast, displays the names of both operators. (Paul Savage)

Heading along Buckingham Palace Road, London, on its way to Victoria Coach Station on National Express route 410 from Wolverhampton, is Travel de Courcey Marcopolo-bodied MAN A91 MD29 (CV09 COV). (K. A. Jenkinson)

Passing through Birmingham on its way to Liverpool is Selwyn of Runcorn's Plaxton Elite-bodied Volvo B9R 142 (YN10 FKO). (K. A. Jenkinson)

Selwyns of Runcorn's Caetano Levante-bodied Scania K340EB4 131 (FJ58 AJU) is adorned with promotional graphics for football at Wembley Stadium. (Les Long)

National Express Caetano Levante-bodied Volvo B9R C114 (FJ60 HXX) is pictured here adorned with promotional graphics in support of the Commonwealth Games held in England. (Gawan Wood)

Heading through Hyde Park Corner, London, on its way to Victoria Coach Station in May 2012 is contractor Yeomans of Hereford's corporate-liveried Caetano-bodied Scania K340EB6 41 (FJ08 KNK). (K. A. Jenkinson)

Circumnavigating Hyde Park Corner in May 2012 and branded for the London to Stansted Airport service is National Express Caetano Levante-bodied Scania K340EB6 SC11 (FN07 BYV). (K. A. Jenkinson)

Seen in Leicester painted in a gold livery in support of the Commonwealth Games in 2012 is National Express Caetano Levante-bodied Volvo B9R SR115 (FJ60 HXY). (Gawan Wood)

Picking up its passengers at Birmingham Airport is National Express Irizar-bodied Scania K114EB4 NXL22 (YN05 WJO), which has its destination aperture externally mounted on its front roof dome. (K. A. Jenkinson)

Leaving Peterborough bus station en route to Grimsby on 14 July 2012 is Stagecoach East National Express liveried Plaxton Elite-bodied Volvo B9R 53709 (AE10 JTV). (D. W. Rhodes)

Leaving Bradford Interchange en route to Glasgow on 14 November 2012 is Parks of Hamilton Plaxton-bodied Volvo B9R KSK986, which is showing a National Express fleet name and promotional graphics for the Pride of Britain awards. (K. A. Jenkinson)

Operating the A1 service between Luton Airport and London in 2014, National Express Caetano Levante-bodied Volvo B9R CA150 (FJ13 EBP) carries branding across its rear side panels and windows and an 'easyBus' logo below its fleet name. (K. A. Jenkinson)

To celebrate the 20th anniversary of Liverpool Coach Station on 20 November 2014, preserved ex-Ribble Duple-bodied Leyland Leopard 1052 (UTF 732M) and Selwyn of Runcorn's Caetano-bodied Volvo B9R FJ13 EBF were displayed to show National Express coaches of a past and present age. (K. A. Jenkinson)

Four of Clarkes of London's Mercedes-Benz Tourismo coaches are seen here at their depot ready for their next duty. (Clarkes)

New to Clarkes, London, in June 2016 was this top-of-the-market Irizar i8, YR16 UCS. (Irizar)

Reversing its ban on double-deck coaches, National Express purchased six Caetano Boa Vista-bodied Scania K410UD6's in October 2016, one of which – CD02 (BV66 WPK) – is pictured here. (Caetano)